100 Questions and Answers About Veterans: A Guide for Civilians

Michigan State University
School of Journalism

Read The Spirit Books

an imprint of
David Crumm Media, LLC
Canton, Michigan

For more information and further discussion, visit
news.jrn.msu.edu/culturalcompetence/

ISBN: 978-1-942011-00-2

Cover art and design by
Rick Nease
www.RickNeaseArt.com

Published by
Read The Spirit Books
an imprint of
David Crumm Media, LLC
42015 Ford Rd., Suite 234
Canton, Michigan, USA

For information about customized editions, bulk purchases
or permissions, contact David Crumm Media, LLC at info@
DavidCrummMedia.com

Contents

Acknowledgments

Michigan State University students who worked on this guide are: Isaac Berkowitz, Madeline Carino, Riccardo Cozzolino, Daniel Hamburg, Tiara Jones, Lia Kamana, Katie Krall, Kary Moyer, David Reiss, Gabriela Saldivia and Darren Weiss.

We had valuable advice and support every step of the way from Detroit Public Television, which also produced the video interviews that appear in this guide. We thank Detroit Public Television President and CEO Rich Homberg, and Senior Vice President for Content and Community Engagement Georgeann Herbert.

Jeff S. Barnes, director of the Michigan Veterans Affairs Agency, also advised us and we had assistance from the agency's Tina Richardson, Randy D. Calloway and Kim Miller.

Several people consulted on the project and helped edit the questions and then the answers. They helped ensure the guide's accuracy and authority. They are:

Nikki G. Bannister served six years and nine months as a gas turbine systems mechanic in the U.S. Navy and is a member of American Legion Post 500. She began her journalism career at Southern University and A&M College in Baton Rouge, Louisiana. There, her coverage of Hurricane Katrina and 18 NCAA Division I sports led to her being named Southeast Journalism Conference 2006 College Journalist of the Year. Her career includes assignments at newspapers in Kentucky and Ohio, along with bylines at more than 10 print and online media outlets including The Advocate (Baton Rouge, Louisiana) and the Times-Picayune (New Orleans). She is the founder and principal editorial consultant of Nik Scott, an "editorial relations" firm.

Cindy Burton was in the U.S. Air Force from 1980 to 1986 (four years active duty, two years reserves). She served as a cryptologist linguist and her language was Arabic. Her last rank was E-5 staff sergeant. She was stationed in Iraklion Air Station, Crete, Greece; and Fort Meade, Maryland, where she worked at the National Security Agency. Burton is accredited with the Department of Veterans Affairs to represent veterans who have been denied benefits. Her son-in-law did two tours of duty in Afghanistan. She has degrees in journalism and law. She was news editor at the Sun News in Myrtle Beach, South Carolina, and managing editor at the Centre Daily Times in Pennsylvania. She has been an editor at the Detroit Free Press for more than 16 years.

Bill Elsen worked for 33 ½ years, primarily as an editor, at The Washington Post. From 1994 to 2001, he was a director of recruiting and hiring for the newsroom. He is an editor for the Newspaper Association of America and the Maynard Institute for Journalism Education. He was also an adjunct faculty member and editor at the Freedom Forum Diversity Institute at Vanderbilt University. He is a former editor and career development director for reznetnews.org, a news, information and entertainment website that trained and mentored Native American college students. Before joining The Post, Elsen was a reporter and copy editor for the Nashville Banner, a sports copy editor for The Tennessean in Nashville and a sports writer and sports editor for the Washington (D.C.) Daily News.

He served in the U.S. Army in Vietnam and was a reporter in Saigon for Stars and Stripes.

Georgeann Herbert grew up in Norfolk, Virginia, where she was the only kid on the block whose family wasn't either in active service with or employed by the U.S. Navy. She worked at the Norfolk Naval Station during the summers while attending the University of Virginia, and covered Navy, Army, Air Force and Coast Guard stories as the military affairs and waterfront beat reporter at WTAR Radio in Norfolk. In the 1990s, she brought her experience working with the military to bear at CBS Radio in Chicago, in reporting on the Desert Storm campaign and as the radio producer and adviser to the Chicago Air and Water Show. Since joining Detroit Public Television in 2010, Herbert has been working with veteran organizations to share Stories of Service for PBS and helping to connect newly separated military personnel to community organizations that help their transition to civilian life.

Lily H. Li credits the U.S. Army for her American citizenship. An elderly maternal uncle who came to these shores before the repeal of the Chinese Exclusion Act served in the armed forces during World War II and decades later sponsored her parents, two brothers and herself for legal immigration and ultimately naturalization. Her journalism career spans nearly 20 years, including stints at The New Yorker, Money, eFinancialCareers.com, The Glass Hammer, Life and Discover as well as Newsday, the Los Angeles Times and the Dow Jones Newswires. She compiled the World Watch and Business & Finance columns at The Wall Street Journal. Its staff won the 2002 Pulitzer Prize for breaking-news reporting of the Sept. 11, 2001, terror attacks.

Brian Mockenhaupt is a contributing editor at Outside and Reader's Digest magazines, and the nonfiction editor at the Journal of Military Experience. He writes regularly for The Atlantic, and his work has appeared in Esquire, Pacific Standard, Backpacker, The New York Times Magazine and

Chicago. He served two tours in Iraq as an infantryman with the 10th Mountain Division. Since leaving the U.S. Army in 2005, he has written extensively on military and veteran affairs, reporting from Afghanistan and Iraq, hometowns and hospitals, and even Mount Kilimanjaro, which he climbed with a former soldier blinded by a bomb in Baghdad. Prior to joining the Army, Mockenhaupt worked as a newspaper reporter in the United States and at The Cambodia Daily, an English-language newspaper, and as a contributing reporter for the Far Eastern Economic Review. He has reported from Cambodia, Burma (Myanmar) and South Korea.

Mark Thompson has been covering national-security issues in Washington, D.C., since 1979, and for Time since 1994. He spent more than a decade covering the wars in Afghanistan and Iraq, as well as the hidden costs of those conflicts—suicide and drug abuse among them—inflicted on some of the veterans who waged them. Before coming to Time, Thompson covered national-security issues for Knight-Ridder newspapers from the capital for eight years. From 1979 to 1985, he reported from Washington for the Fort Worth Star-Telegram, where his reporting on a design problem with Fort Worth-built helicopters won the 1985 Pulitzer Prize for public service.

Sarah Welliver is an award-winning multimedia photojournalist with the Elkhart Truth in Indiana. She has been a staff photographer with the Island Packet in South Carolina and a photojournalism intern with the Santa Fe New Mexican, the Detroit Free Press and the Sioux Falls (South Dakota) Argus Leader. She has also been multimedia mentor to the Native American Journalism Career Conference. Welliver was a sergeant in the U.S. Marine Corps, where she served from 1999 to 2003. Her father was career Army and she had two grandparents who served during World War II.

Dozens of other veterans and civilians helped including Air Force veterans C. Wesley Battoe and Chris King, Marine veteran Charlie Liu of the Michigan State University Office of

International Students and Scholars, MSU students Cheyenne Yost and Cody Harrell and MSU graduate Dmitri Barvinok.

Lucinda Davenport, director of the MSU School of Journalism, has supported this series from the beginning.

About the Series

The Michigan State University School of Journalism publishes this series of guides as a tool to replace bias and stereotypes with accurate information. We create guides that are factual, clear and accessible. We decided to make this guide because of persistent stereotyping about veterans, who number more than 20 million.

We make these guides by asking people to tell us the questions and assumptions they hear about their group in everyday conversations. Some questions are simple, but the answers seldom are.

At times, we must interpret questions to uncover the meaning behind them. We search for answers in studies, surveys, books and research. We ask experts. Our goal is to answer first-level questions in ways that are accurate and clear. We respect the people who ask the questions as well as the people the answers describe.

These 100 questions and answers do not do justice to the variety of perspectives of millions of veterans. While veterans have a shared bond in military service, their experiences are intensely personal and unique. They also represent a true cross section of American perspectives and values. They are as different as they are alike.

Our hope is that you will start with these answers, use the resource section to dig deeper and talk with the veterans you meet. Listen to their stories. Get to know them as the individuals they are. True understanding does not come through 100 questions, or even 1,000, but through one person at a time.

Joe Grimm, series editor, is visiting editor in residence at Michigan State University's School of Journalism.

Foreword

By J.R. Martinez

I'm a son, brother, friend, father, and sometimes I can even be a goofball. That's who veterans are. We are you. The only thing that separates us is that we've decided to join the military and we've experienced things in our line of work that many others have not.

Some people have called me a hero for being in the military. Others have called me a monster for being in the military. I wish people would take the time to listen to me. Maybe eventually they'd just call me J.R.

For many people, military life is completely foreign unless they have a direct connection to it; say, a family member in one of the service branches, or maybe a friend. But less than 0.5 percent of the U.S. population serves in the armed forces. And if you don't know a member of the military or a veteran, it's hard to truly see the differences, and more importantly the similarities, between us and civilians. So how do we bridge that gap of understanding? We are just like you, yet we seem so unfamiliar to so many.

Every day in the news we see a new story about the effects of service-related Post Traumatic Stress and Traumatic Brain Injuries. We see more injured troops returning home. We see military spending cuts. We see homelessness and joblessness among veterans reaching near epidemic proportions.

And at the same time we see stories of escalating conflicts throughout the world, which might mean a need for more boots on the ground. And that will certainly mean more injuries, more casualties, and more troops returning home to see their benefits slashed.

The public sees all of this and might not see it for the growing problem that it is. All it would take is just listening to a veteran or service member. Let yourself learn from us. Ask us questions. Listen and try not to judge or to let your perceptions get in the way of our answers. And in turn, we will allow ourselves to understand that it is our duty to teach. It's a partnership we will all have to agree on to shorten the distance between our two worlds.

J.R. Martinez enlisted in the U.S. Army in 2002 and was deployed to Iraq in 2003. There, the Humvee he was driving hit an improvised explosive device. He suffered smoke inhalation and severe burns to more than 34 percent of his body. He is an actor, motivational speaker and the author of "Full of Heart: My Story of Survival, Strength, and Spirit," Hyperion, 2012.

Preface

By Ron Capps

I suppose the first question is why? Why is this book necessary? Well, how's this for starters: more than 21 million Americans are veterans. That's a pretty good chunk of people. But given our current population of over 320 million, it's perhaps the smallest percentage of the population since the Second World War. Fewer people serve in the military, so fewer Americans really understand the military or those who have served in it.

And there are other questions. The editors here came up with 100, beginning with, "Who is a veteran?" This question is troublesome because there are different answers depending on why one is asking the question.

When the Greeks came home from Troy, people were naturally curious to know what had happened. This was, of course, before Twitter, so no one had been reading their feeds to stay current on the Trojan War. So naturally the first question was, "Who won?" But after that, after the parades and the family reunions, probably after a good meal and some wine, each Greek soldier took part in a ritual telling of his experience. Each soldier stood in the town square or the village amphitheater and, in front of his neighbors, told his story of the war as a way of communalizing the experience of war and of sharing the burden of it.

We don't do a particularly good job of this today. Soldiers come home and get lots of "Thank you for your service" and recognition at baseball games, but rarely have the chance to tell their story. This lack of communication leads to a lack of understanding. Veterans can become isolated, and keep to themselves. And this is wrong. We all have a responsibility to share the experience of our military even if only vicariously, through a telling or a reading.

Why? Because within the small slice of America we think of as our veteran population, all of America is present. There are big-city and small-town veterans, black and white veterans, male and female veterans, straight and gay veterans, young and old veterans.

Like all good books, this one furthers a continuing conversation. In this case, it's a necessary and important conversation about service, values, war, humanity and much more, and we should all take part in it.

Ron Capps served in the Army and Army Reserve for 25 years. He is a veteran of the war in Afghanistan and of numerous other conflicts. Capps founded the Veterans Writing Project (veteranswriting.org) in 2011. He is the author of "Seriously Not All Right: Five Wars in Ten Years," Schaffner Press, 2014.

Demographics

1 Who has veteran status?

This is complicated. Basically, a veteran is someone who served in the active military, naval or air service and was discharged or released under any condition besides dishonorable. This can include members of the Guard or Reserves. Contractors and others who work with the U.S. military do not become veterans because of their work. State and federal agencies have varying standards for determining eligibility for different services and benefits.

2 How many U.S. veterans are there?

According to the U.S. Census Bureau, there were 21.8 million veterans of the U.S. armed forces in 2014. The size and makeup of the veteran population changes as time passes.

3 Which conflict involved the most U.S. service personnel?

World War II involved 16,112,566 U.S. service personnel worldwide, according to the U.S. Department of Veterans Affairs (VA). The next largest were the Vietnam War with 8,744,000 and the Korean War with 5,720,000. Not all service personnel are assigned to combat areas.

4 How many U.S. military deaths have there been in various wars?

Wartime deaths have many causes. They include combat, non-combat injuries, illnesses and accidents. Deaths caused in combat areas do not always occur immediately.

According to federal records:

World War I	**53,402**
World War II	**291,557**
Korean War	**33,741**
Vietnam War	**58,220**
Gulf War (1990-1991)	**147**

According to iCasualties.org:

Afghanistan (2001-2014)	**2,356**
Iraq (2003-2014)	**4,489**

5 In which conflict were the most American lives lost?

The Civil War had the most with an estimated 625,000 deaths, about 2 percent of the population. Civil War fatalities were not as accurately documented as they are today.

6 What percentage of veterans are women, and how is that changing?

The proportion of female veterans has been growing for about three decades. According to the VA, almost 4 percent of U.S. veterans in 1980 were women. That rose to 10 percent in 2015 and will be almost 18 percent by 2040.

7 Are WACS and WAVES veterans?

The Women's Army Corps (WAC) and the Women Accepted for Volunteer Emergency Service (WAVES) are veterans. In May 1941 during World War II, U.S. Rep. Edith Nourse Rogers (R-Mass.) drafted a bill that created a volunteer women's corps for the Army. Members were given military status in 1943 as the Women's Army Corps (WAC). WAVES served in the Navy and, though they were not members of the armed forces, Women Airforce Service Pilots (WASPs) provided support by flying planes. The Marines admitted women in 1943. Approximately 400,000 women served with the armed forces during World War II.

Elaine Homic-Schima
Veteran, United States Army

View video at: http://bit.ly/1JcMH4I

8 What are the racial and ethnic demographics of veterans?

According to the U.S. Census Bureau, this is the distribution:

Caucasian   **80.2 percent**

African American	**11 percent**
Hispanic or Latino	**5.5 percent**
Asian American	**1.2 percent**
American Indian or Alaska Native	**0.7 percent**
Native Hawaiian or Pacific Islander	**0.1 percent**

Military segregation was not abolished until 1948. In World War II, African American Tuskegee Airmen distinguished themselves as pilots. American Indian code talkers representing 13 tribes developed indecipherable codes. The Japanese-American 100th Infantry Battalion and the 442nd Regimental Combat Team was highly decorated. The units earned seven Presidential Unit Citations, two Meritorious Service Plaques, 36 Army Commendation Medals and 87 Division Commendations. Members received 21 Medals of Honor, 29 Distinguished Service Crosses, one Distinguished Service Medal, more than 354 Silver Stars and more than 4,000 Purple Hearts.

9 What was the military's "Don't Ask, Don't Tell" policy?

In 1982, President Ronald Reagan proposed a Department of Defense directive stating, "homosexuality is incompatible with military service." It required that gays, lesbians and bisexuals be discharged from the military if they were discovered. "Don't Ask, Don't Tell" was instituted under the Bill Clinton administration in 1994 and said military applicants should not be questioned about their sexual orientation. The policy was dropped in 2011.

What are the demographics of veterans?

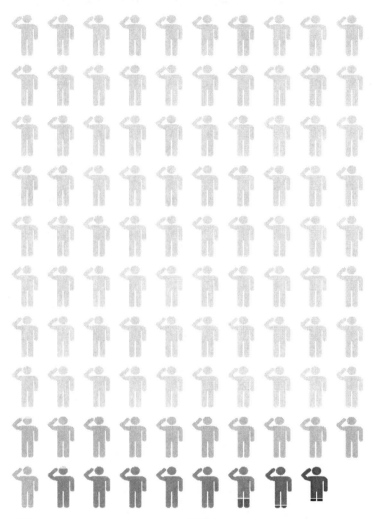

Caucasian: **80.2%**

Asian American: **1.2%**

African American: **11%**

American Indian/Alaska Native: **.7%**

Hispanic/Latino: **5.5%**

Native Hawaiian or Pacific Islander: **.1%**

illustration by Cody T. Harrell

source: U.S. Census Bureau

10 How did things change after "Don't Ask, Don't Tell" was repealed?

One year after the directive was repealed, a study by the UCLA Law School showed no negative consequences from repeal of the policy. Military applicants do not have to disclose their sexual orientation.

Service

11 How did ending the draft in 1973 change the military?

According to the Rand Corporation, the all-volunteer U.S. military grew in part out of Vietnam-era opposition to the draft. A 1970 presidential commission said the draft led to "morale and disciplinary problems that otherwise would not arise." Rand reported that the all-volunteer military meant higher pay and greater professionalism. That, according to Rand, caused a higher rate of reenlistment and a sharp increase in the number of personnel who made the military their career.

12 Why do people go into the military?

Some look for careers in the military. For others, it could be a means to an education or to see the world. The military is a way to serve the country, and people can be especially motivated by times of national crisis, such as World War II or the 9/11 attacks. Some families have legacies of military service that go back generations.

13 What percentage of service personnel serve in combat?

About 33.9 percent of veterans reported having served in combat as of 2010. This is according to the "National Survey of Veterans, Active Duty Service Members, Demobilized National Guard and Reserve Members, Family Members, and Surviving Spouses." It was published by the VA.

14 Do women serve in combat?

From 1994 until 2013, women were allowed to serve in combat zones, but not in combat positions. In 2013, Secretary of Defense Leon Panetta and Chairman of the Joint Chiefs of Staff Gen. Martin Dempsey ended the ban on women in combat. The goal was a fully gender-integrated force by 2016.

Jeff Barnes
Director, Michigan Veterans Affairs Agency
Veteran, United States Army

View video at: http://bit.ly/1JcMIpj

Military Structure

15 What are major differences among the branches?

Each of the five branches of the U.S. military serves a different purpose. Each has active-duty personnel, reserves and veterans.

- The **Air Force** is responsible for air and space. Air Force personnel operate planes, helicopters and satellites.
- The **Army** is the primary land force. It operates tanks and some aircraft.
- **Marines** are the first-response force, trained to arrive by sea and fight on land. They are sometimes called soldier sailors. The Marine Corps has an aviation wing.
- The **Navy** is known for working on the sea but also works on land and in the air.
- The **Coast Guard** works on domestic waters. Personnel in this branch are responsible for rescues and keeping waterways clear. In addition, the Coast Guard enforces law on U.S. waterways.

16 What do we call members of the different branches?

They are airmen, soldiers, Marines, sailors and guardsmen. Members of one branch are not called by names used for members of another.

17 How are commissioned and noncommissioned officers different?

The greatest difference is in level of authority. Commissioned officers can command officers under their authority and all enlisted personnel. Noncommissioned officers do not command commissioned officers except those under their command for training. Because of this, commissioned officers lead larger groups, but they rely heavily on the expertise and leadership of noncommissioned officers under them. Commissioned officers are paid more. Many come from service academies, senior military colleges and maritime academies. Most of these schools grant scholarships in exchange for service.

18 Who commands the military?

The chain of command starts with the president of the United States, who is the **commander in chief**. Next is the **secretary of defense**, a civilian cabinet member appointed by the president and approved by the U.S. Senate. The president, through the defense secretary, orders military actions that are undertaken by the combatant commanders, who are responsible for different regions of the world. The **National Security Council** advises the president and the secretary of defense on national security or foreign policy. Each branch of the military has a chief. These five chiefs, with a chair and vice chair appointed by the president, form the **Joint Chiefs of Staff**. They are military advisers to the president, the secretary of defense and the National Security Council. They are responsible for training and outfitting the nation's military forces.

19 What is military court?

A military court, called a court-martial, is for trying members of the armed forces accused of breaking military law. The Uniform Code of Military Justice provides for three types of courts-martial: summary, special and general. These courts-martial differ in the severity of the charge, the number of court members present and severity of punishment.

20 How is the Uniform Code of Military Justice different from civilian laws?

The Uniform Code of Military Justice details the justice system within the military and criminal offenses under military law. The rules and regulations come from the commander in chief as the Manual for Courts-Martial. People tried in military court do not have all the constitutional protections of civilian systems, the laws can be stricter and the punishments greater. Members of any U.S. armed force, retired members receiving hospital services or pay, and people in the custody of the U.S. military fall under the code. People tried in military court can be additionally charged in civil and criminal courts. All veterans lived under military law while on active duty.

21 What are the highest medals in the different branches?

The highest is the Medal of Honor, which Congress can award to members of any branch of the armed forces. The second highest honor depends on the branch. Army personnel would receive the Distinguished Service Cross.

Personnel in the Navy, the Marine Corps (and the Coast Guard, if acting under the Navy) would receive the Navy Cross. Air Force members would receive the Air Force Cross. The third-highest honor is the Silver Star, which can be awarded to members of any branch.

22 Is it illegal to wear medals one has not earned?

The Stolen Valor Act outlaws false claims of having received certain military decorations if done with the intent of financial gain. Some interpret the idea more broadly and object to any false claim or exaggeration of military service.

23 Does everyone in the military carry a weapon?

No. Most service personnel do not have fighting roles and do not need weapons every day. The United States maintains its military in times of peace, too. Organized under the Department of Defense, the branches are set up to protect or secure the homeland and its interests around the world.

Military Culture

24 Do the military branches have rivalries?

Yes. The primary rivalry is for money from Congress. The second involves pride and the desire to be better, tougher, faster than others. The Army-Navy football game has been held almost every year since 1890. The military tries to manage competition with a focus on the need to work together in the interests of the country.

25 How do job responsibilities vary among branches?

Often, they do not. All branches need medics, cooks, clerks, mechanics and logistics people. While the branches train for different environments such as air, land and sea, few jobs are specific to one environment. Not everyone in the Air Force is a pilot and not everyone in the Navy works on a ship.

26 What do the terms "head," "go fasters," and "moon beam" mean?

This is military jargon. Like any occupation, the military has its own language, which includes thousands of slang terms. They can vary widely from era to era, branch to branch and place to place. They can be a kind of linguistic glue. Some slang is profane, racist or sexist. Some has crossed over into mainstream conversation. The "head" is the latrine or bathroom, "go fasters" are running shoes and a "moon beam" is a flashlight.

27 Why are some veterans so precise about appearance?

This comes from training. Equipment, clothing, even the way military people salute, stand and sit, have evolved over decades of practice. There are reasons behind the tiniest detail. Experience made it what it is; training and discipline ingrain it.

28 Do service members have a sense of camaraderie?

Very much so. Within units, survival depends on individuals' thoughts and actions. Some veterans have shared triumphs or losses that were among the most intense in their lives. No one but them can really appreciate those feelings. It is not uncommon for veterans to feel as close as family members with one another, and some accept each other's families as their own.

29 Are veterans who served in the same branch at different times close?

Yes. Although veterans might not have served together, they still have shared experiences, jargon, understanding and perspectives. It is common for them to ask one another what unit they served in, where and when. If they served at nearly the same time, they likely would know some of the same people. These connections can mean an instant and lifetime bond.

30 What is the goal of basic training, or boot camp?

Besides physical and mental conditioning and evaluation, basic training teaches required discipline, working as part of a unit and following orders precisely. It teaches military practices and culture. Basic training helps to determine how recruits will become part of the culture. It is one of the initial filtering mechanisms.

31 How does being in the military change a person?

This varies. Ingrained behaviors like discipline, precision and teamwork may persist. Veterans who became service personnel at young ages can find afterward that they must start making decisions that had been made for them in the military. Veterans might find a disconnect between military protocol, decision-making and reward systems and the way things are done in the civilian world. For most, military service is a unique, transformative experience whether they speak openly about it with pride or decline to discuss it with civilians.

32 What are the origins of "Reveille" and "Taps"?

These are two of several bugle calls historically used throughout the day. "Reveille" is based on a call dating back to the 17th century Crusades and sounds the beginning of morning roll call and the raising of the flag. "Taps," arranged in 1862 during the Civil War from an older call, signals lights out. It is also played at funeral ceremonies for service personnel and veterans.

Deployment and Discharge

33 How long does enlistment last?

This varies. Enlistment is typically four years of active duty followed by two years on Individual Ready Reserve. There are options for two, three or six years of active duty plus reserve time, or for all reserves. Military personnel can be called from reserves to active duty at any time.

34 What determines deployment length?

Deployment is moving into an area of action, which might not mean combat. An entire unit can be deployed or an individual can be deployed to another unit. Lengths can be as short as a few weeks for special units. Some deployments in Iraq reached 22 months. Average deployment times have been getting shorter and are about a year or less. This is better for troops. Deployments can be ended when the job is done. In October 2014, for example, troops deployed to West Africa to fight the Ebola virus were told to expect to stay for as long as a year. By February 2015, most were returning.

Where do veterans live after service?

Number of veterans by state

- <100K
- 100K - 200K
- 200K - 350K
- 350K - 650K
- 650K - 950K
- 950K>

illustration by Cody T. Harrell
source: Department of Veterans Affairs 2013

Where do military personnel come from?

WA	3,570
OR	2,161
CA	18,987
NV	1,432
ID	994
AK	487
AZ	4,121
UT	1,016
MT	481
WY	266
NM	1,078
CO	2,914
HI	804
ND	169
SD	360
NE	901
KS	1,307
TX	16,078
OK	2,139
MN	1,804
IA	1,272
WI	2,486
MO	3,325
AR	1,456
LA	2,132
MS	1,633
AL	3,124
TN	3,722
IL	5,718
IN	3,338
MI	4,727
KY	1,916
OH	6,151
WV	825
GA	7,387
SC	3,313
NC	6,049
VA	5,252
PA	5,430
FL	12,609
VT	253
NH	723
ME	811
NY	7,681
MA	2,409
CT	1,298
RI	387
NJ	3,326
MD	2,805
DE	419

Veterans by state per year

- <1K
- 1K-3K
- 3K-5K
- 5K-8K
- >8K

illustration by Cody T. Harrell
source: Bureau of Labor Statistics Current Population Survey, 2013

35 Are bonuses offered to induce people to stay in the service?

Sometimes, enlistment and reenlistment bonuses are available. This depends on factors including the branch of service, specialty and length of enlistment. Each branch determines eligibility based on needs.

36 How does pay vary?

It depends on the sector of the military. Pay varies based on factors that include rank, grade and length of time in service.

37 What are base pay and additional pay?

There are two types of basic military pay for enlisted personnel. The main component of an individual's pay is the monthly base, paid according to time in the military and rank. Military allowances pay for specific needs such as food or housing. Base pay is taxed; allowances are not. Additional pay categories include hostile fire, hazardous duty, flight pay, special duty and more.

38 What is the Individual Ready Reserve?

IRR is a source of trained personnel who have left active duty but can be called to service. They keep their rank and uniforms and are supposed to notify the military of their whereabouts. They generally are not paid unless doing military work, and they retain some benefits. Having transitioned out of uniform and moved on with their lives, many do not want to be reactivated or deployed. They can appeal callbacks or ask for deferments. The military frequently grants these requests, but does not have to.

39 How does IRR differ from the Reserves?

IRR is one of several reserve components of the armed forces. Some others, including the National Guard, are designed for civilians or retired military and may require regular, short-term service and offer regular pay. Members of all components can be called into active service.

40 Can veterans re-enlist once discharged?

Re-enlistment is encouraged, depending on the nature of the discharge. Good candidates have the training, experience and aptitude to quickly make new contributions. There are several re-enlistment programs. Some are as short as a year or two and some allow Army and Air Force personnel to join the other branch.

41 What is a DD214?

Also called DD-214, DD Form 214 or just 214, this U.S. Department of Defense document is issued when military personnel retire, separate or are discharged. The certificate identifies the type of discharge and information of interest to employers. One veteran said, "It is an ID card, birth certificate and Social Security card all rolled into one." It can include rank and last assignment, job specialty, military education, decorations, citations and campaign awards.

42 What are the types of discharge?

There are six: honorable, general, other than honorable, bad conduct, dishonorable and entry-level separation. Service personnel who are medically discharged separate under one of these categories. Those who are dishonorably discharged are typically ineligible for veteran benefits.

43 Can you leave the service whenever you want?

Usually not. Service is for a predetermined period, and one cannot leave active duty before completing the enlistment. Early departures must be approved, but they are rare. Some reasons are for education, medical discharge and conscientious objection.

44 Is retiring the same as being discharged?

Not really. One can be discharged from the military after just a few years, but true retirement with pay requires a certain length of service, usually 20 years. Service members can retire from active duty, the Reserve or National Guard. There are provisions for medical retirements.

45 What percentage of military personnel were deployed to Iraq and Afghanistan?

According to a Rand Corporation study, almost four in seven deployments in Iraq and Afghanistan were in the Army. Rand reported that by 2011, roughly 73 percent of soldiers had deployed to Iraq, Afghanistan or both. Most were working on their second, third or fourth year of deployment. Those who had not deployed had supported the missions from the continental United States, were recent recruits, or served in other overseas locations.

46 Has everyone deployed to Iraq or Afghanistan been in combat?

Not all. Many were physicians, mechanics, or information technology specialists, for instance, or served in support positions away from combat areas. Some may have engaged in combat remotely as drone pilots or from vessels at sea.

Benefits

47 What is the role of Veterans Affairs?

The VA is responsible for providing veterans "benefits and services they have earned." Its mission is to "fulfill President Lincoln's promise 'to care for him who shall have borne the battle, and for his widow, and his orphan' by serving and honoring the men and women who are America's Veterans."

48 Who receives veteran benefits and what are they?

Benefits are available to veterans, their spouses, dependents or survivors. They include disability compensation, employment services, home loans and housing-related assistance, education and training, health care, life insurance, a pension and memorial benefits. According to VA documents, the department "provides free health care for veterans who served in a theater of combat operations after Nov. 11, 1998, for any illness possibly related to their service in that theater." However, 55 percent of veterans in a 2014 Gallup Poll said it was very or somewhat difficult to obtain medical care through the VA. The survey was taken after news reports of long delays and inadequate care.

49 What is the GI Bill?

The GI Bill "provides financial support for education and housing to individuals with at least 90 days of aggregate service on or after Sept. 11, 2001, or individuals discharged with a service-connected disability after 30 days." The bill provides as many as 36 months of education. Veterans' children can receive tuition for in-state public schools and a monthly housing allowance. Veterans who do not use post-9/11 benefits may transfer them to their spouse or children. Benefits have changed over time, so veterans of different eras receive different levels of support.

50 Are veterans paid after their service ends?

Like millions of civilian employees, veterans' pensions are based on age or disability. Surviving spouses and children are also eligible for assistance if they meet income and net-worth limitations. According to the VA website, 308,116 veterans and 210,450 survivors received pension benefits in 2013. Pensions are paid only to those who served 20 or more years and retired. Disability benefits, which are different from pensions, are paid to a veteran who was injured because of military service.

51 How does the type of discharge affect benefits?

A veteran with an honorable or general discharge is eligible for most benefits. These will not be available with an other-than-honorable discharge, but the VA examines the circumstances to determine eligibility. With a bad-conduct discharge, a veteran is generally ineligible for benefits. Through a special judicial proceeding, the VA can determine whether a veteran should receive some benefits. If a veteran is convicted at a general court-martial and receives a dishonorable discharge, all benefits are lost. Entry-level separations are rare and given only within the first 180 days of service. No benefits are earned with this discharge.

52 Are there special benefits for wounded or injured veterans?

Wounded, ill and injured military personnel and their families may be eligible for specific pay and entitlements. They include assistance with daily living activities, concurrent retirement and disability pay, combat-related compensation and transfer of GI Bill benefits. Traumatic Injury Protection benefits are for losses including amputations; paralysis; burns; loss of sight, hearing or speech; facial reconstruction; coma; and loss of activities of daily living due to traumatic brain injury. Like civilians, injured veterans are also eligible for Social Security disability.

53 Are there special benefits for female veterans?

Women are entitled to the same benefits. Gender-specific medical services are also available, including breast and pelvic examinations and preventive care such as contraceptive services, menopause management, Pap smears, reproductive counseling and mammography. The VA's Center for Women Veterans monitors and coordinates administration of benefit services and programs for female veterans.

54 Are there benefits for families of those killed on active duty?

Spouses, children and parents of service personnel who die while on active duty receive burial benefits, dependency and indemnity compensation and life insurance. The VA offers a Casualty Assistance Program that gives personal attention to surviving family members after in-service deaths to help with benefit information and applications. TRICARE, a health-care program for almost 9.5 million beneficiaries worldwide, is offered to active-duty service members, their families, survivors, certain former spouses and others registered in the Defense Enrollment Eligibility Reporting System. Educational assistance is available to spouses and children under certain circumstances.

55 Are there death benefits?

Yes. These can include help for families, burial costs, burial in a military cemetery, a military funeral and a flag. Benefits vary by branch of service, type of discharge and other factors. Discharge papers are needed to secure benefits. Each branch keeps copies at the National Personnel Record Center in St. Louis.

Education

56 What training comes after basic training?

Basic training is just the start. After that, each branch has specialized and technical training for jobs that need to be filled. Further training can be voluntary or mandatory. Training is often a requirement for a service member to receive higher levels of pay or promotions. Finally, there is training for the transition back to civilian life.

57 Can veterans receive college credit for what they learned in the service?

Yes. The American Council on Education was established in 1942 to help recognize the educational value of military training and experience. ACE can help veterans earn a degree based on occupational specialty, training and coursework.

58 Are there scholarships or educational aid for veterans?

The federal government and nonprofit organizations offer college assistance to veterans, future military, active-duty personnel and those related to veterans or active-duty personnel. There are scholarship opportunities for veterans or their families, depending on the branch and where and when the veteran served. Children of veterans do not receive free education.

59 How many veterans attend college after serving?

Studies have shown that about half of veterans eligible for the GI Bill after World War II obtained a training certificate or college education, and about two-thirds of Vietnam veterans did. More than half of veterans who went to school under the GI Bill from 2002 to 2013 completed their schooling, according to a review of 800,000 academic records released in 2014. The number of veterans seeking educational opportunities had more than doubled in the previous decade. The most popular fields of study now are business, social sciences, homeland security, law enforcement and firefighting, and computer and information services.

Employment

60 What are employment statistics for veterans?

The unemployment rate for veterans improved in 2013, declining to 6.6 percent, slightly lower than the overall national unemployment rate. The rate for female veterans was 6.9 percent. The rate for those who had been on active duty at any time since September 2001 declined to 9 percent in 2013. Statistics are from the U.S. Department of Labor's Bureau of Labor Statistics.

61 What advantages do veterans bring to the civilian job market?

Military training can instill important workplace skills such as leadership, discipline, dependability, teamwork and taking responsibility. Certain job classifications may align with similar civilian jobs. For other veterans, a careful analysis of their military work record and skills can help match them with civilian jobs.

How do veterans fare economically?

Veterans annual income (wages, Social Security, retirement pensions, VA payments, and other forms of income) is $10,000 higher than the average American.

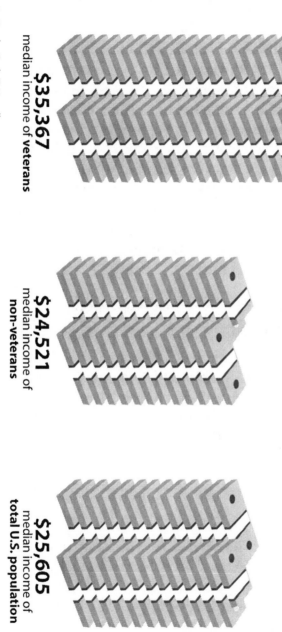

$35,367
median income of **veterans**

$24,521
median income of
non-veterans

$25,605
median income of
total U.S. population

illustration by Cody T. Harrell
source: Census Bureau 2010

⟩⟩ $1,000 in income

62 What challenges do veterans face in the job market?

A veteran's résumé does not look like a standard civilian résumé and might not match civilian job requirements. Specialized military training might not seem to translate as readily as civilian experience or a college education. Furthermore, some veterans do not have much experience applying for jobs, and negative stereotypes about how well veterans adjust to civilian workplaces can also be factors. There exists a significant cultural gap between military and civilian work settings. Training, certification and length of service that lead to promotions or raises in the military matter less in most civilian workplaces.

63 In what private-sector fields or functions do veterans often find work?

According to a 2014 study, the 15 top employers of veterans included government agencies and companies dealing with weapons, security, aerospace and information technology. The study was conducted by Forbes magazine and the compensation site Payscale.com.

64 What other industries are veteran friendly?

Each November, G.I. Jobs publishes a list of the 100 "most military friendly employers." In 2014, the list included Combined Insurance, Deloitte, Pacific Gas and Electric Co., American Electric Power Co., Goodyear Tire & Rubber Co., Eaton Corp., United Rentals and The Home Depot.

65 How do civilian employers support veteran employees?

One strategy is for a company to have a veterans employee resource group, or a supportive community of veterans within the company. Veterans working in a company may help screen applicants for jobs to help translate job skills for open positions. Most importantly, veterans within a company can "buddy up" with new veteran employees and help them transition to the corporate world.

66 Could veterans have had more than one specialty or job in the military?

Certainly. They can be trained for varied responsibilities within one job and take additional training for others. Service personnel are tested and assigned to training and work, but these can be varied despite narrow descriptions, and assignments change.

67 Do veterans make good leaders and managers?

It seems so. A U.S. Census Bureau report showed that the percentage of veterans in management and professional occupations in 2012 was higher than the percentage for non-veterans. For men, the proportion in such jobs was 34.2 percent for veterans compared with 32.7 percent for non-veterans. For women, the difference was greater, with 47.3 percent of female veterans in leadership roles compared with 39.6 percent of civilian women.

68 Do veterans start their own businesses?

The National Veteran-Owned Business Association reports that about 25 percent of military veterans own businesses, compared with approximately 9 percent of non-veterans. The study did not include retired people. The U.S. Small Business Association has an Office of Veterans Business Development, and other organizations run programs to help veterans start businesses.

69 How do veterans fare economically?

The U.S. Census Bureau reports that veterans do better than non-veterans in terms of median earnings and personal income. The advantage for female veterans compared to other women is greater than the comparison for males.

View video at: http://bit.ly/1JcMHkY

Military Families

70 Do military couples marry young?

Military sociologist Jacey Eckhart studied 1,200 long-married, active-duty Army, Navy, Air Force, Marine Corps and Coast Guard couples. She found that their average age of marriage was 22, about four years younger than the civilian average. Many couples marry right before deployment in case anything should happen to the active-duty spouse.

71 Is divorce higher among military couples?

Veterans have a higher divorce rate than non-veterans. One indicator of divorce is early marriage, and divorce rates decline as people age. Deployments and other responsibilities play a large role. Frequent relocations and family separations are sources of stress for military families that may lead to divorce.

72 Do military families move frequently?

Researcher Eckhart found that military couples moved an average of 8.6 times in 20 years. Most children in the study attended six to nine schools between kindergarten and 12th grade, according to an article posted by the National Military Family Association.

73 What effects do deployments have on children?

This was studied by an American Psychological Association task force. According to the VA's National Center for PTSD, the task force found that reactions vary, but "Very young children may exhibit separation anxiety, temper tantrums, and changes in eating habits. School-age children may experience a decline in academic performance and have mood changes or physical complaints. Adolescents may become angry and act out, or withdraw and show signs of apathy."

74 Do some veterans find it hard to reconnect after absences?

Each family handles the stress of returning differently. Most need time to readjust to home and family life. Usually the most stressful time can be the first few months, when it's most difficult for families to understand what their veteran is experiencing. Most returning service personnel and veterans make the switch successfully.

75 What family issues arise when someone returns to civilian life?

Big issues involve recovering from an injury. Small issues can include moving from an oft-regimented life to one in which there are many routine decisions to make. Other changes can include living under a new set of rules, having new responsibilities or adjusting to a life that is not as exciting or adrenaline-filled.

Transitions

76 What are challenges veterans face while transitioning to civilian life?

A Pew Research Center study found that 72 percent of veterans of different age groups reported adjusting easily. Those who reported difficulty cited several patterns. Most were related to combat. These included experiencing a traumatic event; having a serious injury; being a post-9/11 veteran, especially if married while serving; being in combat; or knowing someone who was killed or injured.

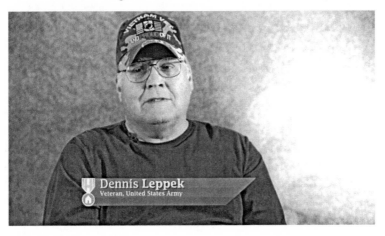

Dennis Leppek
Veteran, United States Army

View video at: http://bit.ly/1JcMIFB

77 What programs does the military offer to help people re-acclimate?

The U.S. Department of Defense's Transition GPS (Goals, Plans, Successes) has four major components:

- Mandatory pre-separation counseling conducted by the military services
- A U.S. Department of Labor three-day employment workshop
- Individual Transition Plan Review
- Benefits briefings sponsored by the VA

78 Why do some veterans decline to discuss their experiences?

There is no single answer. Some took an oath not to talk about their work because of security clearances. Others have had their sense of global security changed and do not want to burden others with that. Some were deeply affected by their experiences and do not want to relive them. Still others just want to move on and not be defined or judged by experiences that most civilians might not understand. But do ask. Veterans would rather have people ask than to make assumptions about their service. They are comfortable telling people when they do not want answer a question. Do not let that discourage you from asking.

What are challenges of transitioning to civilian life?

According to The Pew Research Center, more than seven in ten veterans (72 percent) reported they had an easy time readjusting to civilian life and 27 percent said re-entry was difficult. Pew researchers analyzed the attitudes, experiences and demographic characteristics of veterans and examined the impact on re-entry of 18 demographic and attitudinal variables. They found four variables that significantly increased the likelihood that a veteran would have an easier time readjusting to civilian life. Six factors predicted a more difficult re-entry experience.

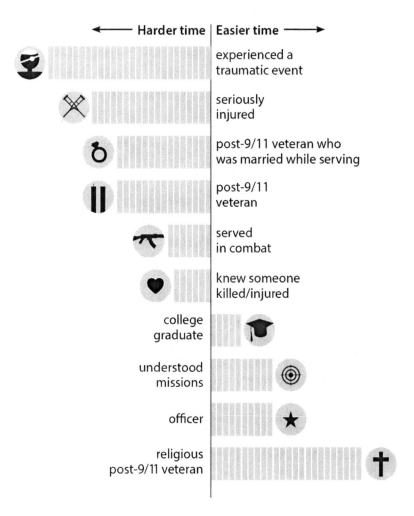

◀— Harder time | Easier time —▶

experienced a traumatic event

seriously injured

post-9/11 veteran who was married while serving

post-9/11 veteran

served in combat

knew someone killed/injured

college graduate

understood missions

officer

religious post-9/11 veteran

illustration by Cody T. Harrell
source: The Pew Research Center, 2011

79 What do Memorial Day and Veterans Day commemorate?

In May 1868, the head of an organization of Union veterans — the Grand Army of the Republic — established May 30 as Decoration Day, a time to decorate the graves of the war dead with flowers. By the end of the century, Memorial Day was being recognized throughout the country. Memorial Day is for mourning those who have died in military service. Saying "Happy Memorial Day" is out of step. Some confuse Memorial Day with Veterans Day, which honors veterans. Originally called Armistice Day, Veterans Day marks the end of World War I fighting at 11 a.m. Nov. 11, 1918: the 11th hour of the 11th day of the 11th month.

80 Why do some veterans object when thanked for their service?

Sometimes, a civilian will say "Thank you for your service" to a veteran without knowing what that service might have been. Although well intentioned, the remark can sound superficial, much like "Have a nice day." Some veterans may wish civilians would put words into action and support. It is probably safest not to assume that the veteran you just met would appreciate a hearty thank-you. Each veteran will interpret his or her service differently. It can be especially awkward to thank a veteran on Memorial Day, which is not for recognizing the living.

Challenges

81 What is PTSD?

Post-traumatic stress disorder, or simply post-traumatic stress, as some call it, can occur after experiencing an event that is harmful or potentially harmful to someone or those nearby. There are four types of reactions. They are: reliving the trauma; avoiding situations that recall it; negative changes in beliefs, feelings or thoughts; and always feeling on edge.

Troy Schielein
Director, Wayne County Veterans Affairs
Veteran, United States Marine Corps

View video at: http://bit.ly/1JcMHl0

82 How common is PTSD among veterans?

According to the VA, 11 percent to 20 percent of veterans of operations Iraqi Freedom and Enduring Freedom experience PTSD each year. For the Persian Gulf War, this proportion is about 12 percent and for the Vietnam War about 15 percent.

83 Do non-veterans experience PTSD?

Yes. According to the VA's National Center for PTSD, 60 percent of all men and half of all women experience trauma at least once. A center report says, "Women are more likely to experience sexual assault and child sexual abuse. Men are more likely to experience accidents, physical assault, combat, disaster, or to witness death or injury." The center estimates that about 5.2 million Americans, 7 percent to 8 percent of adults, will experience PTSD during their lives.

84 Are there other chronic military-related health conditions?

Yes. One is from Gulf War oil well fires. There are traumatic brain injuries. The VA considers all Vietnam War and Korean War veterans to have been exposed to the herbicide Agent Orange and to be eligible for benefits. Additionally, studies suggest that the risk of breast cancer among female veterans is 20 percent to 40 percent higher than for civilian women. Rising injury-survival rates, attributed to better care, mean more veterans with serious injuries, including amputations and brain damage.

85 Do veterans have higher rates of alcohol and drug abuse?

Studies have shown that alcohol and prescription drug abuse is higher among military personnel and veterans, but that the use of illegal drugs is lower. A 2012 National Institute on Alcohol Abuse and Alcoholism report said that alcohol abuse occurs among a substantial proportion of combat veterans coping with PSTD. This type of self-medication impedes their recovery. A 2013 report by the National Institute on Drug Abuse said that while military personnel were less likely than civilians to use illegal drugs, abuse of prescription drugs was higher and growing.

86 What is the link between military service and suicide?

A 2014 report by the National Institute of Mental Health said that although suicide death rates in the Army had been lower than those for civilians, they began climbing in the 2000s and exceeded the civilian rate in 2008. A 2013 report by the Journal of the American Medical Association showed that military suicides do not necessarily correlate to military-specific variables such as combat experience or days deployed. Suicides can occur or be attempted for reasons unrelated to service.

87 How prevalent is sexual trauma among veterans?

The VA frequently asks male and female veterans if they have experienced military sexual trauma. This is defined as sexual assault or repeated, threatening acts of sexual harassment. According to the 2014 survey, one in four women and one in 100 men indicated they had experienced military sexual trauma.

88 How have civilian attitudes toward veterans changed?

Research done from 1972 to 2011 by the Pew Research Center showed an increase in public confidence in the military, with 80 percent of civilians reporting that they had a "great deal of confidence." Seventy percent reported they had thanked someone in the military, and 90 percent indicated they had pride in their troops. Pew also reported that 84 percent of veterans believe that the public does not understand the problems faced by those in the military. Civilians agreed, with 71 percent reporting that they did not understand what military service is like.

What are civilian attitudes toward veterans?

80% of civilians confident in the military

70% of civilians have thanked someone in the military

90% of civilians report having pride in their troops

84% of veterans believe civilians don't understand problems they face

71% of civilians report they don't understand what it's like to have served

illustration by Cody T. Harrell
source: The Pew Research Center, 2011

89 How can civilians support veterans?

This is a good way to think about the issue. Not all veterans want or need help. Many veterans help civilians. Supporting an individual veteran begins with paying attention and listening. To support veterans in general, contact a group that works with them. Veterans have established many groups, and several are in the resource section at the end of this guide.

90 How do I know whether veterans organizations are legitimate?

Many have established groups to support veterans. Even some that are well intended might not be effective. There is no fail-safe way to know whether an organization or non-profit claiming to help veterans is legitimate. You must do research. Talk to veterans you know, find information online, check organizations' tax status and use websites such as charitynavigator.org and organizations like the Better Business Bureau that do credibility checks.

Stereotypes

91 Are veterans heroes?

Labels such as "hero" and "warrior" frequently are used to describe a veteran's service. Veterans themselves are not often looking for these labels, nor do they feel labels accurately portray their service. Some veterans served in support roles that did not require heroism. Other veterans who might have done remarkable things say their actions were just part of the job or their only choice. As members of a unit that went into combat together, some are uncomfortable with being singled out for acclaim. Others have regrets about things they did not or could not do.

92 Why are there homeless veterans?

According to the website of the National Coalition for Homeless Veterans, "a large number of displaced and at-risk veterans live with lingering effects of post-traumatic stress disorder and substance abuse, which are compounded by a lack of family and social support networks." These factors combine with the difficulty some veterans have in finding jobs. Moreover, they can encounter a lack of affordable housing or medical care and jobs that pay well.

93 How prevalent is this problem?

The U.S. Department of Housing and Urban Development estimates that about 50,000 veterans are homeless on any given day. That is about 12 percent of the total adult homeless population but only about one in every 500 veterans.

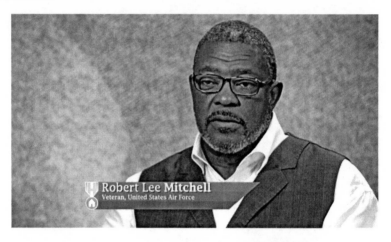

Robert Lee Mitchell
Veteran, United States Air Force

View video at: http://bit.ly/1F3hl1P

94 Veterans are sometimes portrayed as damaged. Is this common?

Physical, mental and moral damage is real. However, this is not the case for most veterans, and injury is just one dimension of a person. These portrayals are often featured in pop culture and generate sympathetic news coverage. Some veterans who have experienced injury say they have emerged stronger than ever and do not wish to be pitied. Most veterans are healthy and not easily distinguished from civilians.

Politics

95 Do most veterans share the same political beliefs?

Military service is only one dimension of a veteran's political makeup. Other important factors are age, race, where and how they were raised and beliefs they held before beginning service. A 2011 report by the Pew Research Center on social and demographic trends said post-9/11 veterans are more likely than adults overall to identify with the Republican Party. Thirty-six percent of veterans identified as Republicans, compared with 23 percent of adults generally. Twenty-one percent of post-9/11 veterans called themselves Democrats while 34 percent of the electorate identified that way. About 35 percent of veterans and nonveterans identified as independents. Other studies say former military officers, who make up about 17 percent of veterans, are more likely than other veterans to lean Republican.

96 Is there a veterans voting bloc?

Because the nation's 22 million veterans make up 10 percent of the electorate, they could wield some clout. In general, however, they do not vote as a bloc, although they do share interests in defense issues and veterans benefits. Candidates seeking to attract veterans do make appeals to them.

97 Do veterans generally support the president's military policies?

Whether or not they agree with the policies, active service members must obey the orders of the commander in chief. After discharge, veterans are free to agree or disagree, a basic American right that the military helps to protect. While in uniform, military personnel are barred under the Uniform Code of Military Justice from expressing strong opinions.

98 What are some legislative actions that affect veterans?

Several were being debated in early 2015. One is the Mobile Medical Homeless Health Improvement Act of 2013, which aims to improve medical care for homeless veterans. The Homes for Heroes Act of 2013 establishes special assistance to veterans struggling to find permanent homes. The Military Family Home Protection Act of 2013 offers help finding homes to disabled veterans and surviving family members of those killed in combat.

99 How prominent are veterans in American politics?

Of the 535 members in the 113th Congress (2013-2014), 108 had served or were serving in the military, according to "Membership of the 113th Congress: A Profile," published by the Congressional Research Service in 2014. The two female veterans were combat veterans. The highest number of veterans recorded was during the 95th Congress (1977-1978) during which 77 percent of members had served, according to the Pew Research Center. More than half of

U.S. presidents served in the armed forces, and 24 were in combat. The most recent president with combat service was George H.W. Bush, a Navy pilot in World War II and president from 1989 to 1993. Veterans and their advocates told USA Today that they face more challenges running for office today.

100 How can I learn more?

Good question. We suggest you get to know the veterans around you. Listen with an open mind. Because each veteran has his or her own perspectives and views, listen to many. The following resources can help, too.

U.S. ARMY

OFFICERS

 General of the Army

 General

 Lieutenant General

 Major General

 Brigadier General

 Colonel

 Lieutenant Colonel

 Major

 Captain

 First Lieutenant

 Second Lieutenant

 Chief Warrant Officer 5

Chief Warrant Officer 4

Chief Warrant Officer 3

Chief Warrant Officer 2

Warrant Officer

ENLISTED

 Sergeant Major of the Army

 Command Sergeant Major

 Sergeant Major

 First Sergeant

 Master Sergeant

 Sergeant First Class

 Staff Sergeant

 Sergeant

 Corporal

 Specialist

 Private First Class

 Private 2

NONE   Private

U.S. AIR FORCE

OFFICERS		ENLISTED	
	General of the Air Force		Chief Master Sergeant of the Air Force
	General		Command Chief Master Sergeant
	Lieutenant General		Chief Master Sergeant (Diamond)
	Major General		Chief Master Sergeant
	Brigadier General		Senior Master Sergeant (Diamond)
	Colonel		Senior Master Sergeant
	Lieutenant Colonel		Master Sergeant (Diamond)
	Major		Master Sergeant
	Captain		Technical Sergeant
	First Lieutenant		Staff Sergeant
	Second Lieutenant		Senior Airman
			Airman First Class
			Airman
		NONE	Airman Basic

U.S. MARINE CORPS

OFFICERS

☆☆☆☆	General
☆☆☆	Lieutenant General
☆☆	Major General
☆	Brigadier General
	Colonel
	Lieutenant Colonel
	Major
	Captain
	First Lieutenant
	Second Lieutenant
	Chief Warrant Officer 5
	Chief Warrant Officer 4
	Chief Warrant Officer 3
	Chief Warrant Officer 2
	Warrant Officer

ENLISTED

	Sergeant Major of the Marine Corps
	Sergeant Major
	Master Gunnery Sergeant
	First Sergeant
	Master Sergeant
	Gunnery Sergeant
	Staff Sergeant
	Sergeant
	Corporal
	Lance Corporal
	Private First Class
NONE	Private

U.S. NAVY

OFFICERS		ENLISTED	
	Fleet Admiral		Master Chief Petty Officer of the Navy
	Admiral Chief of Naval Ops		Fleet/Commander Master Chief Petty Officer
	Vice Admiral		Master Chief Petty Officer
	Rear Admiral		Senior Chief Petty Officer
	Rear Admiral		Chief Petty Officer
	Captain		Petty Officer 1st Class
	Commander		Petty Officer 2nd Class
	Lieutenant Commander		Petty Officer 3rd Class
	Lieutenant		Seaman
	Lieutenant Junior Grade		Seaman Apprentice
	Ensign		NONE Seaman Recruit
	Chief Warrant Officer 5		
	Chief Warrant Officer 4		
	Chief Warrant Officer 3		
	Chief Warrant Officer 2		

illustrations by Cody T. Harrell
source: U.S. Military

U.S. COAST GUARD

OFFICERS

 Admiral Chief of Naval Ops/ Commandant of CG

 Vice Admiral

 Rear Admiral

 Rear Admiral

 Captain

 Commander

 Lieutenant Commander

 Lieutenant

 Lieutenant Junior Grade

 Ensign

 Chief Warrant Officer 4

 Chief Warrant Officer 3

 Chief Warrant Officer 2

ENLISTED

 Master Chief Petty Officer of the Coast Guard

 Command Master Chief Petty Officer

Master Chief Petty Officer

Senior Chief Petty Officer

Chief Petty Officer

Petty Officer 1st Class

Petty Officer 2nd Class

Petty Officer 3rd Class

Airman

Fireman

Seaman

Airman Apprentice

Fireman Apprentice

Seaman Apprentice

Seaman Recruit

illustrations by Cody T. Harrell
source: U.S. Military

Resources

Books by veterans can be a way to go in-depth on one person's experiences and perspective. These are some recent books:

Abrams, David. *Fobbit*. New York: Grove Press' Black Cat, 2012.

Busch, Benjamin. *Dust to Dust: A Memoir*. New York: Ecco Press, 2012.

Buzzell, Colby. *My War: Killing Time in Iraq*. New York: Berkley Books, 2006.

Campbell, Donovan: *Joker One: A Marine Platoon's Story of Courage, Leadership, and Brotherhood*. New York: Random House, 2010.

Castner, Brian. *The Long Walk: A Story of War and the Life That Follows*. New York: Anchor, 2013.

Fick, Nathaniel. *One Bullet Away*. New York: Mariner Books, 2006.

Gallagher, Matt. *Kaboom: Embracing the Suck in a Savage Little War*. Boston: Da Capo Press, 2011.

Johnson, Shoshana, with M.L. Doyle. *I'm Still Standing: From Captive U.S. Soldier to Free Citizen—My Journey Home*. New York: Touchstone Books, 2011.

Kraft, Heidi Squier. *Rule Number Two: Lessons I Learned in a Combat Hospital*. New York: Little, Brown and Company, 2007.

Luttrell, Marcus, with James D. Hornfischer. *Service: A Navy SEAL at War*. New York: Back Bay Books, 2014.

Powers, Kevin. *The Yellow Birds*. New York: Back Bay Books, 2013.

Turner, Brian. *Here, Bullet*. Farmington, Maine: Alice James Books, 2005.

Van Winkle, Clint. *Soft Spots: A Marine's Memoir of Combat and Post-Traumatic Stress Disorder*. New York: St. Martin's Griffin, 2010.

West, Owen. *The Snake Eaters: Counterinsurgency Advisors in Combat*. New York: Simon & Schuster, 2013.

Young, Thomas. *The Mullah's Storm*. New York: Berkley Books, 2010.

Movies

Periodically, usually around Veterans Day, some news media publish lists of military movies. The Military Officers Association of America published some picks by military people, and panned some suggested by the media.

In an article for the association, Mark Cantrell asked, "do inaccuracies in military movies really matter? Yes, say veterans, because motion pictures play a large part in forming civilian perceptions of the military." Military people made their own lists, both good and bad. The article said, "There is one thing most service member movie buffs agree on: If Hollywood directors want to show what military life is really like, all they have to do is ask a service member."

Predictably, movies liked by some military movie buffs were disliked by others. These are some that made only the thumbs-up lists:

Act of Valor, 2012
Black Hawk Down, 2001
Courage Under Fire, 1996
Das Boot, 1981
The Deer Hunter, 1978
From Here to Eternity, 1953
Lone Survivor, 2012
Patton, 1970
The Sand Pebbles, 1966
Saving Private Ryan, 1998
The Steel Helmet, 1951
Zero Dark Thirty, 2012

Organizations

There are scores of organizations for and of veterans. These include government agencies in every state and organizations and associations in thousands of cities. The places listed here help civilians learn more about veterans.

American Women Veterans, americanwomenveterans.org
Betty H. Carter Women Veterans Historical Project, libcdm1.uncg.edu/cdm/landingpage/collection/WVHP/
Disabled American Veterans, www.dav.org/
Institute for Veterans and Military Families, vets.syr.edu/
National Veterans Art Museum, www.nvam.org/
Pritzker Military Museum and Library, www.pritzkermilitary.org/explore/veterans-information-center/
Student Veterans of America, www.studentveterans.org/
Team Rubicon, www.teamrubiconusa.org/
Veterans History Project, www.loc.gov/vets/vets-home.html
Veterans Writing Project, veteranswriting.org
Vietnam Veterans Memorial Fund, www.vvmf.org/
Wounded Warrior Project, www.woundedwarriorproject.org/